All I Need

by Deb Loughead

Illustrated by Mary Camozzi

Moonstruck Press
1998

Dedication

For my Mom, Laurie Symsyk, who instilled in me a love of words D. L.

For my husband, David, who lives with an artist! M.C.

First published in 1998
Second printing, 1999

MOONSTRUCK PRESS
17 Thornly Crescent,
Etobicoke, Ontario
M9B 2M4

Canadian Cataloguing in Publication Data

Loughead, Deb, 1955-
All I need

Cover title: All I need and other poems for kids.
ISBN 0-9682680-0-5

1. Children's poetry, Canadian (English) - 20th century.* I. Camozzi, Mary. II. Title.

PS8573.O8634A84 1999 jC811'.54 C99-931943-4
PZ7.L68A1 1999

All I Need

I left my footprints
on the moon
just sitting in my chair,
I snorkeled in
a coral reef,
and never wet my hair.

I met a giant
in the woods,
and didn't run away,
I rode a horse
to Camelot,
it only took a day.

I tumbled down
a rabbit hole,
and wasn't scared at all,
I balanced on a
tightrope and
was sure I wouldn't fall.

I flew across
the galaxy
but never left the ground,
I lost myself
inside a cave,
and knew that I'd be found.

I battled
ancient warriors
while curled up in bed,
I searched a
magic wardrobe
in a land inside my head.

When I crave
a new adventure,
a book is all I need!
I've seen it all,
I've done it all,
because I learned to read.

Elephant Walk

An elephant went for
a walk down my street,
he stamped and he tramped
with his wrinkly feet,
he stepped on the flowers,
he flattened the trees,
he knocked over shrubs
with his grey saggy knees,
he used someone's car
as an elephant seat
and the pool in the park
to cool off in the heat,
all the dogs started howling,
he frightened the cats,
he stretched out his trunk
to snatch grandmothers' hats,
then he sprayed all the kids
with a trunkful of water
and gave a quick ride
to the mayor's young daughter,
he cracked all the sidewalks
and buckled the street,
then he trampled away
on those wide, stumpy feet.

Stink Stank Stunk

Stink stank stunk,
I would love to pat a skunk.
Such furry pretty creatures,
with their dainty kitty features.
Pyjama striped in black and white,
sneaking through the yard at night.
Stink stank stunk,
how I'd love to pat a skunk...

But I must steer clear
of that stinky spray,
for if, by chance,
I got in the way,
I'd have to bury my
clothes in the yard,
and sleep outside
with the St. Bernard,
and soak in tomato
juice all day,
until the skunk smell
went away!

Stink stank stunk.
I won't ever pat a skunk!

Ants

Cross-eyed ants never stop

racing in crazy zigzags,

scurrying over furrows,

zipping across the sidewalk,

stumbling over tufts of grass,

tripping into tunnels underground...

how do they know their way around?

Scritchy Scratchy

Lying on a hilltop,
in the summer sun,
watching as the clouds pass,
counting every one.

Something starts to tickle,
something I can't see,
pretty soon I'm scratching
every part of me!

Wiggling, jiggling, jumping,
scratching everywhere,
Itchy arms and itchy legs
and even itchy hair!

Itchy scritchy scratchy,
each and every part–
lying on an ant hill
isn't very smart!

Dust Bunnies

If I open my bedroom door
too quickly,
my dust bunnies scatter,
afraid it might be Mom,
planning a surprise attack!
Off they go,
scuttling under the dresser
and the bed,
hurry scurrying into the closet
and creeping into corners
where her vacuum cleaner
can't reach them.

Sometimes I help them hide,
scooping them into my slippers
and tucking them
under the mat
where Mom can't capture them.

My dust bunnies don't eat much.
Just bits of fluff
and lint and stuff–
such quiet, wispy pets,
and easy-care.
But for some reason,
my Mom can't stand them
one
little
bit!

Our House

When I'm in bed at night and I hear creaking,
I know it's just the sound of our house speaking.

It whispers to the houses on our street
about the constant thumping of our feet,

And how we wipe our fingers on the walls,
and race our cars and trucks along the halls,

Our noses always smudging window panes,
the carpets always splotched with spills and stains.

Perhaps our house is planning an escape,
because we never keep it quite in shape.

One morning we might all wake up to find,
our beds are all the house has left behind.

Our house will find itself a vacant lot,
and settle its foundation on that spot,

Then shut its window eyes and lock its door,
so children can't mistreat it any more!

The Moon Came Out

The moon came out
the other night,
and sailed across the sky,

It looked just like
a shiny charm,
and made me wish that I

Could pluck it from
the velvet dark
and tuck it in my pocket,

Or hang it on
a silver chain,
and wear it like a locket.

When a Storm

When a storm comes grumbling
down the sky
and swarms around my house,
I run and hide.

It rattles the windows
and shakes the shutters,
trying its best
to get inside.

But it can't,
so it huffs and puffs and rants,
with flashing eyes
it mumbles and chants,

and swirls around
the foundation outside,
trying to take my house
for a windy ride!

Puddle Day

I love a rainy puddle day,
just kicking up my heels,
and splashing til I'm drippy wet,
I love the way it feels.

And sinking in the puddle mud,
until my boots are gone,
then tugging hard to pull them out,
and keep my stockings on!

And marching with the raindrops,
in step along the street,
parading through the puddles
to the pitter patter beat.

And when I've had enough of rain,
I step inside the door,
and then, just like a cloud, I leave
a puddle on the floor.

Tug-O-War

Sometimes mud can steal your boot.
It grabs hold
when you're strolling along,
and yanks it
right off your foot.
You have to fight
to get it back,
balancing on one boot,
and pulling hard on the other
in a tug-o-war
with the earth.
If you tug hard enough,
the mud gives up
with a sudden slurp,
and you stumble–
then it tries to steal your sock!

Like a Weed

The other day my mother said
I'm growing like a weed!
A weed!
Can you imagine!
That's just what I don't need.

The weeds that I know best of all
are twisted, wild and reedy,
with fuzzy tops,
like dandelions,
spindly and seedy.

What if I turn out like crabgrass,
and spread myself around,
a nasty,
choking weediness
that creeps along the ground.

I hope it isn't ragweed
I resemble most.
Oh please!
Imagine growing like a plant
that always
makes me sneeze!

Maybe I'll be lucky
and grow up
like Queen Anne's lace,
with solid roots, a slender stem,
a sort of
gangling grace.

First Fish

The first time I felt the tug
of a fish on my line,
I let out a shout–
"Look out, this fish is mine!"

Oh ho! It put up a
mighty fight,
splashing at the surface,
then diving out of sight.

"It's yours," my brother yelled,
"Don't let it get away!
You've caught your very
first fish today."

And I hung on even though
my reel kept spinning,
then it slowed down,
and I thought, "I'm winning!"

Then my fish jumped
and it gleamed in the sun,
and a rainbow flashed
on my very first one.

Then it dove back in
and the line went slack.
My brother yelled, "Reel!
Keep fighting back!"

And I tried, but that rainbow
flashed in my mind,
and my hand couldn't get
my reel to wind.

So I stood on the dock
on that sunny day,
and I laughed as my first fish
swam away!

Sea Gulls

Spinning
and twirling,
skimming and swirling,
fluttering flashes of white,
Looping and wheeling, swoopin
and reeling, to dizzy, bedazzlin
heights, flapping and skipping,
diving and dipping,
like so many
runaway
k
i
t
e
s.

Cavendish Beach

Rolling down sand dunes
on Cavendish beach,
the sun in my eyes
and the sand in my teeth,
the hermit crabs scurrying
over the dunes,
the jellyfish stranded
like broken balloons,
the gulls turning cartwheels
over the sea,
the waves doing somersaults
better than me,
the treasures washed up
from the deep ocean floor,
so much to see
and so much to explore,
the wind tossing handfuls
of sand in my face...
I never have seen
such a wonderful place!

Foot Steps

When I wade
in shallow waves
along the beach,
the ocean licks my toes,
wraps its salty tongue
around my ankles,
tries its best
to nuzzle my knees,
makes me freeze!

Three
steps
away,
I sink in hot sand,
shuffle along
through shifty dunes
that smother my feet
with a searing hug,
til my toasted soles
can't stand the heat.

Three

giant

leaps
and they sizzle
in the shallows
along the lapping shore,
icy cold once more.

Summertime is
fun time for my feet,
where sand and water meet.

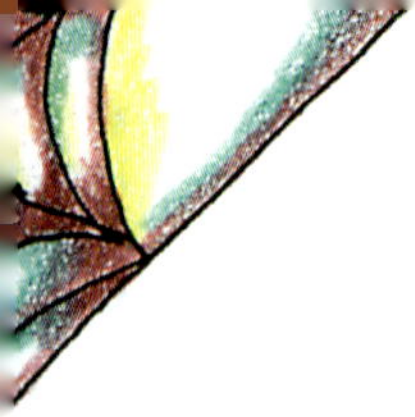

Grandma's Cellar Door

Grandma has a feather mattress
thirty centimetres thick,
an owl-shaped umbrella stand
to hold her walking stick.

Grandma has a cluttered attic
that's just lovely to explore...
but in her cozy kitchen,
she has a cellar door.

She keeps carrots and potatoes
somewhere down there in the gloom,
and cabbages and apples
in her musty storage room.

And the steps are always creaking
even when there's no one there,
as if there's something lurking
in the shadows on the stair.

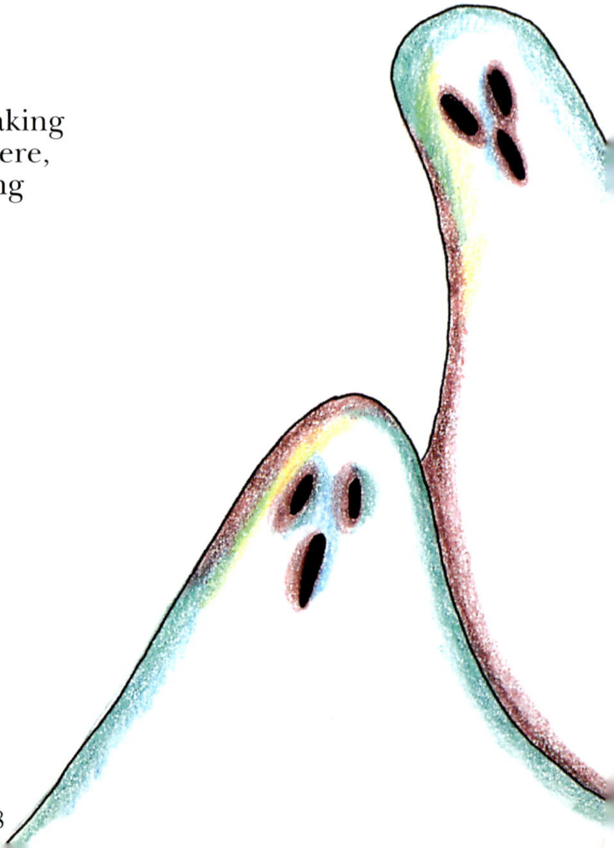

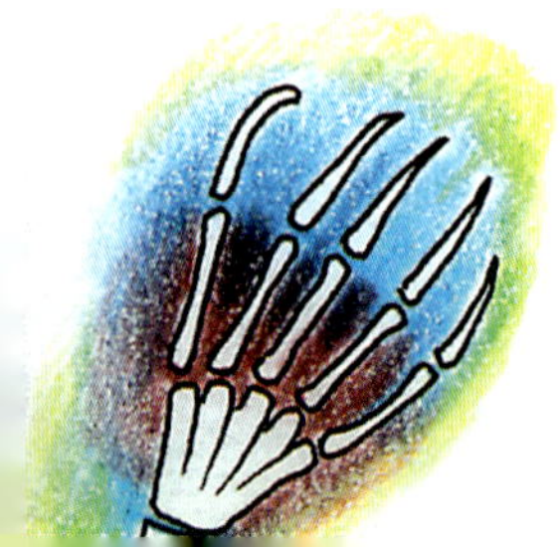

And the dark is always seeping
from underneath the crack,
and stretching spooky fingers
to try to drag me back.

And my Grandma always asks me,
"Are you ready, little feller?
It's time to go downstairs and
fetch the carrots from the cellar!"

Wake-up Ca(w)ll

CAW!

At dawn,
a crowd of rowdy crows
is circling my house,
a chorus of noisy voices
feather-flapping in the pearly light,
shattering my sleep
like a broken plate.

I bury my head
under my pillow and hum,
try to muffle
their crazy serenade,
wonder how they can be so lively
at five a.m., then try
to fall asleep again.

But that raucous racket
is my wake-up call,
and my mood is set
for the day,
black and nasty and rude
as the crows that
splintered my sleep,
reeled in squawking circles
around my house,
wouldn't fly away.

Later I find
a few black feathers
scattered on the lawn.
More proof that
those reckless crows
party far too hard
at dawn!

In the Sky

Sailboats floating
on foamy blue seas,
billowing pillows
that grow in the breeze,

Buckets of popcorn
and candy floss treats,
snowmen and snowbanks
and solid grey sheets,

Galloping stallions
and smiling dogs,
fluffy white kittens
and leap-frogging frogs,

Fluttering feathers
or ghosts drifting by,
so many pictures
to see in the sky!

Creepy Crawly Caterpillar

Creepy crawly caterpillar,
won't you come in my direction,
I'd like to get a closer look,
to give you an inspection.

I hear those fuzzy tufts of yours
could make me start to scratch,
and those spots upon your back
disguise you, like a false mustache.

You're a funny, furry creature,
gobbling up your leafy luncheon.
If I lean a little closer,
I can almost hear you munchin' !

But I think I'll keep my distance,
I don't trust those fuzzy tufts.
With all of my mosquito bites,
I think I itch enough!

Small Wonders

I wonder about
the small things that I see,
the ants that scurry across my shoe,
the spider webs beaded
with morning dew.
And ladybugs with tiny spots,
themselves a lot
like tiny dots.

I wonder about
the dancing fireflies
that flicker on a summer night,
like starlight in the skies,
and bumblebees that rumble
from flower to flower,
so much power
in those tiny wings,
amazing fuzzy things!

I wonder about the inchworms
dangling from a tree
on threads so fine,
they're invisible to me.
And fleas, small bugs with big bites,
like stowaways on furry ships,
always taking trips!

I wonder about the planets
spinning out in space
all the tiny, distant ones
in a far off place
that I can't see–
and I wonder,
is there someone out there,
somewhere,
watching and
wondering
about
me?

Autumn Leaves

Golden leaves
letting
go
spinning, f
a
l
l
ing,

s c a t t e r b l o wwwwww

crispy crunching
under
foot,

kicking, jumping
h
g
i
tossing h

l i
raking, p i n g, light a fire,

smoky plumes in autumn sky.

October Coats

You silly sugar maple tree,
throwing away your leaves,
tossing them into the autumn wind,
and clogging up the eaves.

Just when the air turns frosty cold,
you stand there, bare and tall,
stripped of your bright October coat,
when you need it most of all.

I'm bundled in a coat and hat,
with a scarf around my nose,
and you can be sure you won't catch me
throwing away my clothes!

Dark Things

When night creeps in
the dark things come...
and bedrooms fill with shadows,
spilling into gloomy pools,
waiting there to swallow you.
The dark things seem to seep
beneath the door,
stretching ghostly limbs
across the floor.

Corners soften into smudges,
hazy gray,
where it's so easy to lose your way.
And underneath your bed
the dark things wait in caverns deep,
until you've gone to sleep,
then uncurl spindly fingers
and pinch your hands and feet.

But when closet doors are open
just a crack,
there's room enough for dark things
to sneak back and hide,
when dawn decides
to chase them all
into a darker place.

Something In the Trash

Clatter rattle crash...
There's something in the trash!
I'm all alone. I'm on my own.
Clatter rattle crash!

If I could just be brave enough,
I'd slip into my jacket,
then step outside the door to see
what's making all the racket.

But what if there's a creature there,
with three eyes and a tail,
and spikes and warts and slimy skin
inside my garbage pail?

Or even worse, a zombie,
searching for a place to hide,
and when I open up the door
he'll try to slip inside.

It might be a raccoon out there,
just scrounging for a snack...
but I won't open up the door,
and risk a ghoul attack!

Rumble bumble bash...
There's something in the trash.
I'm safe inside–I think I'll hide!
Rumble bumble bash!

My Cat Doesn't Like Me

My cat doesn't like me,
I just know it,
or maybe she doesn't
know how to show it.
She hisses and thrashes
her thorny claws
and tries to bite
with whiskery jaws.
She flattens her ears
and puffs up her tail,
and then my cat
lets out a wail...
and acts as if
I really bug her,
when all I'm trying to do
is hug her!

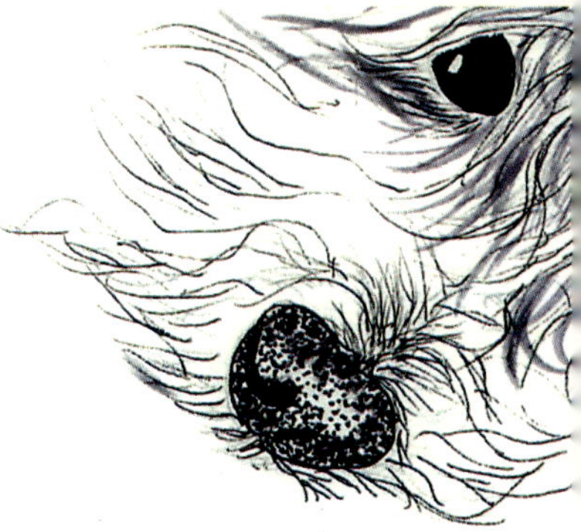

My Dog's Nose

Sometimes my dog's nose
presses against my cheek,
stamping a wet hello,
or rushes along,
hung low,
sucking up smells
on the lawn
like a vacuum cleaner.
She holds it high in the air,
periscope up,
and captures some scent
on the wind,
or squashes it into
the open window's crack
on country car rides,
inhales the smells
of cow pastures
and curling brooks,
then leaves behind
wet sniff prints,
like snail trails
on the glass.

A Million Snowflakes

A million snowflakes fell today,
a million bits of lace,
they tumbled from the winter sky,
and softly brushed my face.

A million graceful dancers,
they came spinning through the air,
twirling in circles
and sticking to my hair.

A million tiny feathers shaken
from an angel's wings,
dropping gently to the earth,
to blanket everything.

A million frosty blossoms
falling from a snowflake tree,
to cover rooftops, streets and yards,
and all that I could see.

I watched a million snowflakes
til the yard was white and new,
and before long I was covered
in a million snowflakes, too!

A Chance of Snow

There's a chance of snow,
my father said,
A chance of flurries tonight.
Well, it's trying to snow,
my mother said,
And the ground is turning white.

Let's hope it holds off,
my father said,
I'm not ready for winter yet.
Yes, let's just hope,
my mother said,
That some flurries is all we'll get.

A chance of snow,
my sister said,
I wonder if it might?
It's trying to snow,
I said to her,
And the ground is turning white!

I hope it snows,
my sister said,
Deep and sparkling bright!
I hope so too,
I whispered back,
I hope it snows all night!

Snowy Days

On snowy days
it's hard to walk,
I have to march and
lift my feet,

lift them high
above the snow,
as I go stomping
through the street.

I have to tramp,
I have to stamp,
and make a pathway
as I go,

and when my legs
get really tired,
I make an angel in
the snow!

And There'll Be Clowns

We're going to the Santa Claus parade.
That jolly old elf, himself,
is coming to town,

And there'll be brassy marching bands
and flashy floats
parading up the streets and down,

Kids decked out in costumes
shiny bright,
and there'll be clowns...

What if a clown
walks up to me today?
Should I turn my head
and look the other way?
What if I can't think
of anything to say?
Whoever thought a goofy clown
could ruin a perfect day?